This copy of

The Fish and Chips
Joke Book

belongs to

_____

Also available by Ian Rylett

Yo Ho Ho! The Pirate Joke Book
The Biggest Smallest Joke Book

THE

fish and chips

JOKE BOOK

Ian Rylett

Illustrated by Ian McGill

RED FOX

A Red Fox Book

Published by Random Century Children's Books
20 Vauxhall Bridge Road, London SW1V 2SA

A division of the Random Century Group

London Melbourne Sydney Auckland
Johannesburg and agencies throughout the world

First published by Red Fox 1992

1 3 5 7 9 10 8 6 4 2

Set in Century Schoolbook
Typeset by JH Graphics Ltd, Reading

Printed and bound in Great Britain by
Cox & Wyman Ltd, Reading

ISBN 0 09 995040 5

Contents

Fish and Chips

BENNY: Why are you baiting your hook with mice?
LENNY: *Because I'm trying to catch catfish.*

Why are chippies mean?
Because their job makes them sell-fish.

How many chips can you get in an empty bag?
One — after that it's no longer empty.

What part of a fish weighs the most?
The scales.

Knock, knock!
Who's there?
Arthur.
Arthur who?
Arthur any scraps left?

SUSIE: I wonder what this cod would say if it could talk?
LUCY: *It would probably say 'Excuse me, but I'm a haddock.'*

Where do fish wash?
In the river basin.

Where should you take a baby fish?
To plaice school.

FREDDY: I went fishing with my wife yesterday.
TOMMY: *Did you catch anything?*
FREDDY: No, so I'm going back to using worms.

How do fish get into business?
They start on a small scale.

Recommended Reading: *Healthier Chips* by Lena Fat.

Where was the chippy when the lights went out?
In the dark.

Why did the little old lady keep her pet fish in a bird-cage?
Because it was a perch.

Knock, knock!
Who's there?
Ivor.
Ivor who?
Ivor forgotten what I came for.

How do you catch an electric eel?
With a lightning rod.

Did you hear about the two fish who kept fighting?
The cod got battered.

WOMAN: Can I have a bag of chips for my son, please?
CHIPPY: *I'm sorry, madam, but we don't do swaps.*

What do you get if you cross a cod with two elephants?
A pair of swimming trunks.

What did the chippy say when the octopus asked for a job?
'You must be squidding.'

How do fishermen make their nets?
They make lots of holes and join them together with string.

MAN: This goldfish you sold me is always asleep.
PET SHOP OWNER: *That's not a goldfish — it's a kipper.*

How do you communicate with a fish?
Drop him a line.

Knock, knock!
Who's there?
Owl.
Owl who?
Owl I get my chips if you don't let me in?

What type of monk goes to the chip shop?
A chip-monk.

How do you get a shellfish up a cliff?
Oyster up.

What two fish are needed to make a shoe?
A sole and an eel.

Knock, knock!
Who's there?
Wendy.
Wendy who?
Wendy fat's hot put de chips in.

Recommended Reading: *My New Business* by Jonah Chippy.

Did you hear about the five-tonne sardine?
It takes some swallowing.

Why are fish clever?
Because they spend all their lives in schools.

Why wouldn't the Chippy sell doughnuts?
Because he was tired of the whole business.

What looks like half a chip?
The other half.

Do fish get colds?
Yes — but only on a small scale.

Knock, knock!
Who's there?
Lettuce.
Lettuce who?
Lettuce in, I'm hungry.

What fish do dogs chase?
Catfish.

MOLLY: You shouldn't eat junk food — they say it's habit forming.
POLLY: *Nonsense — I've been eating it for years.*

What's the difference between a schoolboy and a fisherman?
One hates his books, the other baits his hooks.

Why did the lobster blush?
Because the sea weed.

Why did the fish cross the ocean?
To get to the other tide.

Recommended Reading: *Whale And Chips* by Isa Hungry.

What do sea monsters like to eat?
Fish and ships.

What do musicians like to eat with their chips?
Tuna fish.

What do you get if you cross a pound of potatoes with Adam and Eve?
A chip shop that's never clothed.

What do you call a foreign body in a chip pan?
An Unidentified Frying Object.

How do monsters eat their chips?
By goblin.

TEACHER: Order, children, order!
PUPIL: *Fish and chips thirty times, please!*

Recommended Reading: *Junk Food* by Egon Chips.

Where would you find the chippy's temple?
On the side of his head.

What are hot, greasy and very romantic?
Chips that pass in the night.

What do police fish ride in?
Squid cars.

'Doctor, doctor, I think I need glasses.'
'You certainly do – this is a fish and chip shop.'

How do you deter thieves at a fish and chip shop?
With a burger alarm.

Which fish terrorizes other fish?
Jack the Kipper.

Recommended Reading: *I Love Chips* by Constance Fryer.

What do atomic scientists like for lunch?
Fission chips.

What's the difference between a teletext
television and a newspaper?
*You can't wrap your fish and chips in a teletext
television.*

Recommended Reading: *The Polite Chippy* by
L. O. Customer.

Where do you weigh a whale?
At a whale-weigh station.

MOTHER: Why is your face all burned?
DAUGHTER: *I was bobbing for chips.*

BOY: Fish and chips twice, please.
CHIPPY: *OK, OK, I heard you the first time.*

Where were chips first fried?
In Greece.

Recommended Reading: *The Best Chips in Town* by Trudy Light.

What's the best day to go to the fish and chip shop?
Fri-day.

Can mushy peas get married?
Only if they're Batchelors.

KAREN: My chips taste funny.
DARREN: *That's because you're eating them out of a comic.*

Knock, knock!
Who's there?
Doris.
Doris who?
Doris locked — let me in.

What type of fish lives at the ice-rink?
A skate.

Recommended Reading: *Frying Tonight* by Ivor Chippy.

Frogs' Legs

Why can't frogs get life insurance?
Because they croak every night.

What is a frog's favourite flower?
A croakus.

Where do tadpoles change into frogs?
In the croakroom.

What did the choking frog say to the toad?
'I must have a human in my throat.'

What do toads use when it's foggy?
Frog-horns.

What is the best year for frogs?
Leap years.

Did you hear about the stupid caterpillar?
It turned into a frog.

What is small and green and travels at 150 mph?
A frog in a Porsche.

What is green and stands in the corner?
A naughty frog.

Why is a tadpole like a penny?
Because it has a head on one side and a tail on the other.

'Doctor, doctor, I keep thinking I'm a frog.'
'How long have you been like this?'
'Ever since I was a tadpole.'

How do frogs cross the road?
They use the Green Cross Toad.

What kind of biscuits do frogs like?
Croakers.

What is round, green and smells?
Kermit the Frog's bottom.

What is small and green and has eight wheels?
A frog on rollerskates.

What did the big toad say to the little toad?
'One more game of leap-frog and I'll croak.'

Why did the frog go into hospital?
To have a hoperation.

Why didn't the tadpole believe what the shark said?
It sounded a little too fishy.

'Waiter, waiter, what's this frog doing in my alphabet soup?
'Learning to read.'

How do frogs make beer?
They start with hops.

What do frogs drink?
Croaka Cola.

What happens if you cross a frog with the galaxy?
You get star warts.

Recommended Reading: *Frogs In The Lake* by Lily Pond.

What should you do with a green frog?
Teach it something.

What happened when the two frogs got married?
They lived hoppily ever after.

What is small and green and wears sunglasses?
A frog on holiday.

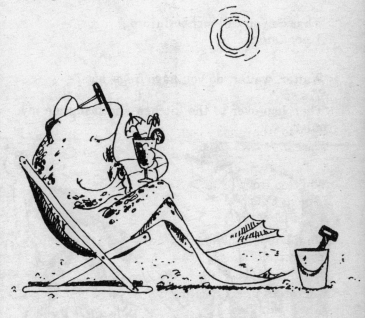

FREDDY: Grandad, do you do frog impressions?
GRANDPA: *No, Freddy. Why do you ask?*
FREDDY: Because Dad says we'll be rich when you croak.

What is white and green and hops across the table?
A frog sandwich.

What is white and green and stays where it's put?
Half a frog sandwich.

Where do frogs keep their money?
In the riverbank.

What do you call a cheerful frog?
A hoptimist.

'Waiter, waiter, do you have frogs' legs?'
'Yes sir.'
'Then hop over to the kitchen and bring me my order.'

What goes 'dot-dot, croak-croak'?
A Morse toad.

What is small and green and drinks out of the wrong side of a glass?
A frog with hiccups.

What happens when frogs park their cars on double yellow lines?
They get toad away.

What did the frog say to the naughty toad?
'Hop it!'

What is small and green and goes 'beep-beep'?
A frog in a traffic jam.

'Waiter, waiter, there's a frog in my soup.'
'Well tell him to hop it.'

What type of story do frogs like?
Croak and dagger ones.

Where does a frog with bad eyesight go?
To the hoptician.

What is a tadpole after it is one week old?
Two weeks old.

What goes 'cloak-cloak'?
A Chinese frog.

'Why did you put a frog in your sister's bed?'
'Because I couldn't find a cobra.'

What is red, green and very sloppy?
A frog in a liquidizer.

'Waiter, waiter, do you have frogs' legs?'
'No, sir, I always walk like this.'

Food for Thought

Why is Europe like a frying pan?
Because it has Greece at the bottom.

What vegetable would you find at the jewellers'?
A carrot.

How can you tell the difference between a can of
tomato soup and a can of chicken soup?
Read the label.

How do you stop a cockerel crowing on Monday?
Eat him for dinner on Sunday.

How do you milk a mouse?
You can't — the bucket won't fit under it.

Did you hear about the carrot that died?
There was a big turnip at the funeral.

What do you call a cow eating grass?
A *lawn-mooer.*

What kind of tree do chickens grow on?
A *poul-tree.*

CUSTOMER: A pair of kippers, please.
FISHMONGER: *I'm sorry, but we don't have a pair left.*
CUSTOMER: That's OK, just give me two odd ones — the wife will never know the difference.

TEACHER: Can anyone tell me why I put my hand over my mouth when I cough?
CHEEKY CHARLIE: *To catch your teeth.*

Did you hear about the hyena that was crossed with an Oxo cube?
He made a laughing stock of himself.

Did you hear the one about the egg?
It's a very funny yolk.

What did the sausage say to the ketchup?
'Don't be so saucy.'

Which cake wanted to rule the world?
Attila the Bun.

What is sweet, covered in custard and very bad-tempered?
Apple grumble.

'Doctor, doctor, I keep feeling like a soft drink.'
'I told you not to play squash.'

'Doctor, doctor, I think I need something for my liver.'
'How about a pound of onions?'

What do joggers like to eat?
Runner beans.

KELLY: Mum, why can't we have a dustbin like everyone else?
MOTHER: *Shut up and keep eating.*

What do ghosts like to drink on a hot day?
Ice-goul demonade.

What do cats like for breakfast?
Mice Krispies.

How do bad drivers lose weight?
They go on a crash diet.

Where did the baby ear of corn come from?
The stalk brought it.

What do mermaids like for breakfast?
Mermalade on toast.

What does the Queen do when she belches?
She issues a royal pardon.

Why did the whale let Jonah go?
Because he couldn't stomach him.

Why wasn't the astronaut hungry?
Because he'd just had a big launch.

What do you get from nervous cows?
Milk shakes.

What do ducks like to eat?
Quackers.

What do you get if you cross a dog with a hen?
Pooched eggs.

Knock, knock!
Who's there?
Butcher.
Butcher who?
Butcher left leg in, your left leg out . . .

What did the fast tomato say to the slow tomato?
'You go on ahead and I'll ketchup.'

Did you hear about the Irish dog who lay down to chew a bone?
When he got up he only had three legs.

What cheese is made backwards?
Edam.

Why did the apple go to the doctor?
Because he wasn't peeling well.

TIM: I've cured my son of biting his nails.
TOM: *How did you manage that?*
TIM: I've pulled all his teeth out.

Why did the lollipop give up boxing?
Because he was always getting licked.

What do hedgehogs eat with cheese?
Prickled onions.

TEACHER: Name six things that contain milk.
PAULINE: *Cheese, butter, yogurt and three cows.*

Why do hungry people go to the desert?
Because of the sand which is there.

Why did the idiot eat little pieces of metal all day long?
Because he heard that a staple diet was good for you.

JACK: If I eat this rotten egg, will it kill me?
JOCK: *Yes — you would be egg-sterminated.*

Did you hear about the idiot who couldn't tell putty from porridge?
All his windows fell out.

What is the fastest vegetable in the world?
A runner bean.

What has one horn and gives milk?
A milk float.

Recommended Reading: *Feed The Baby* by Elsie Cries.

What did the sausage say when he was about to be put on a cocktail stick?
'Spear me, spear me.'

Have you heard the joke about the butter?
Never mind – I don't want you to spread it around.

Which dog has no tail?
A hot dog.

TRACY: Our dog's very friendly – he'll eat off your hand.
LACY: *That's what I'm afraid of.*

Why was the monk covered in lard?
Because he was a friar.

What did the mother biscuit say when her baby was run over?
'Oh crumbs!'

Why did the cannibal feel sick after eating the missionary?
Because you can't keep a good man down.

HUSBAND (LATE HOME FROM WORK): Is my dinner still hot?
WIFE: *It should be – I threw it on the fire an hour ago.*

Recommended Reading: *Maggots in My Salad* by I. Scream.

What is a cannibal's favourite stew?
One with plenty of body in it.

How do witches drink their tea?
With cups and sorcerers.

Knock, knock!
Who's there?
Ice-cream.
Ice-cream who?
Ice-cream if you don't let me in.

Why do maggots like chewing-gum?
Because they're wrigglies.

How do dinner ladies keep flies out of the kitchen?
By dumping a load of manure in the dining-room.

Why did the boy call his dog Sandwich?
Because he was half bread.

What do cornflakes wear on their feet?
Kelloggs.

What did the cannibal say when he saw Santa?
'Yum, yum, Christmas dinner.'

What should you give an injured lemon?
Lemonade.

How do you make and orange cordial?
Give her a mink coat.

What is green and white and bounces?
A spring onion.

Where do chickens go when they die?
To oven.

FREDDY: Please, miss — I don't like cheese with holes.
TEACHER: *Well, just eat the cheese and leave the holes at the side of your plate.*

TIMMY: Please, miss — I've just swallowed my pen. What should I do?
TEACHER: *Use a pencil until the doctor gets here.*

JENNY (CRYING): I've just baked a cake and the cat's eaten it.
KENNY: *Never mind — Dad will buy us a new cat.*

What do cannibals like for supper?
Baked beings on toast.

What illness do kettles suffer from?
Boils.

What's the best thing to put into a pie?
Your teeth.

What's the best way to cure acid indigestion?
Stop drinking acid.

What makes the tower of Pisa lean?
It doesn't eat much.

What did the beaver say to the tree?
'It's been nice gnawing you.'

TOMMY: Please, miss, may I leave the table?
TEACHER: *Well, you can't take it with you.*

What is a sick joke?
Something you shouldn't bring up at dinner.

What type of clothing do you make from old tea bags?
Baggy T-shirts.

What is white on the outside, yellow on the inside and wriggles?
A maggot sandwich.

How do you cool a hot dog down?
Serve it uith chilli.

Why isn't there much honey in Bridlington?
Because there's only one B in Bridlington.

Recommended Reading: *Cooking At Camp* By
Peter Out.

What did the big strawberry say to the little
strawberry?
How ever did we get into this jam?

Why did the one-eyed chicken cross the road?
To get to the Bird's Eye shop.

STEWARDESS (TO CANNIBAL): Would you like to
   see the menu?
CANNIBAL: *No, thank you, just bring me the
   passenger list.*

Who lives in a pod and is a karate expert?
Bruce Pea.

HEEEYA!

What is Dracula's favourite coffee?
De-coffin-ated.

What's the best way to avoid catching diseases
from biting insects?
Don't bite any insects.

LARRY: Our dinner lady was sacked yesterday.
GARY: *What for?*
LARRY: For good.

What's the best way to catch a squirrel?
Climb up a tree and act like a nut.

What is a boxer's favourite drink?
Punch.

How did the carpenter break his teeth?
Because he chewed his nails.

What do you get if you cross a cat with a yogurt?
A sourpuss.

What did the cannibal say when he saw a man sleeping?
'Ah, breakfast in bed.'

What do you call two rows of cabbages?
A dual cabbageway.

LARRY: Does your mum cook best by gas or electricity?
BARRY: *I don't know — I've never tried to cook her.*

'Doctor, doctor, I keep thinking I'm an orange.'
'Well, come a little closer — I won't bite you.'

TIMMY: You still owe me for that honey.
JENNY: *What honey?*
TIMMY: I never knew you cared.

Who invented spaghetti?
Someone who used his noodle.

What did the lion eat after his teeth were pulled
out?
The dentist.

JENNY: Yesterday my mum gave my dad soap
  flakes instead of cornflakes.
PENNY: *Was he angry?*
JENNY: Angry? He was foaming at the mouth!

Why are tonsils so unhappy?
Because they're always down in the mouth.

SALLY: Can I have some of your doughnut?
BILLY: *Yes, you can have the hole in the middle.*

Why did the tomato blush?
Because it saw the salad dressing.

Why are vampires so thin?
Because they eat necks to nothing.

Did you hear about the dog who drank thirty
bowls of water?
He created a new lap record.

What vegetable do plumbers like?
Leeks.

1ST CANNIBAL: We had burglars last night.
2ND CANNIBAL: *Did you?*
1ST CANNIBAL: Yes — it made a change from
  missionary pie.

Why did the hen complain?
Because she was tired of working for chicken feed.

Waiter, Waiter . . .

'Waiter, waiter, what do you recommend for lunch?'
'The café next door.'

Knock, knock!
Who's there?
Howard.
Howard who?
Howard you like to take my order?

'Waiter, waiter, are you in the union?
'Yes, sir — I'm the chop steward.'

'Waiter, waiter, this egg is bad!'
'Don't blame me, sir — I only laid the table.'

Why are waiters' fingers never more than eleven inches long?
Because if they were twelve inches long they'd be a foot.

'Waiter, waiter, this meat pie tastes funny.'
'Then why aren't you laughing, sir?'

'Waiter, waiter, there's a worm on my plate!'
'That's your sausage, sir.'

'Waiter, waiter, there's soap in my soup!'
'That's to help wash it down, sir.'

FRED: This restaurant has no menu. How do we know what there is to eat?
TED: *You just look at the tablecloth.*

Knock, knock!
Who's there?
Roland.
Roland who?
Roland butter, please.

Knock, knock!
Who's there?
Harry.
Harry who?
Harry up with my order.

Why are waiters good at sums?
Because they know their tables.

What did the waiter say when a ghost asked for a glass of whisky to go with his meal?
'I'm sorry, but we don't serve spirits.'

Knock, knock.
Who's there?
Hammond.
Hammond who?
Hammond eggs, please.

Recommended Reading: *The World's Worst Restaurant* by M. T. Caff.

CUSTOMER: Waiter, waiter, this crab has only one claw.
WAITER: *I expect it's been in a fight, sir.*
CUSTOMER: Then take it away and bring me the winner.

Knock, knock!
Who's there?
Butter.
Butter who?
Butter hurry up or we'll be late for the restaurant.

'Waiter, waiter, there's a hand in my soup.'
'That's not your soup — it's the finger bowl.'

SAMMY: Do you know a restaurant where we can eat dirt cheap?
DANNY: *Who wants to eat dirt?*

Why did the apple turnover?
Because it saw the banana split.

'Waiter, waiter, there are feathers in my custard.'
'That's because it's Bird's custard.'

'Waiter, waiter, there's a maggot in my salad.'
'Thank your lucky stars it isn't half a maggot!'

Knock, knock!
Who's there?
Cereal.
Cereal who?
Cereal pleasure to meet you.

Knock, knock!
Who's there?
Pudding.
Pudding who?
Pudding on your hat when it's raining is a good idea.

'Waiter, waiter, my plate is all wet!'
'That's your soup, sir.'

CUSTOMER: Is that roast pork I smell?
WAITER: *It is, and you do* .

'Waiter, waiter, bring me a rotting meat sandwich.'
'I'm sorry, sir, but we're clean out of bread.'

Knock, knock!
Who's there?
Spook.
Spook who?
Spooketti bolognese.

'Waiter, waiter, there's a button in my salad.'
'It must be from the salad dressing.'

'Waiter, waiter, there's another button in my salad.'
'Yes, sir — that will be from the jacket potato.'

What do lions like to eat at restaurants?
The customers.

What do you call a man with a restaurant on his head?
Dead.

'Waiter, waiter, my food is all mashed up.'
'Well, you did ask me to step on it.'

Recommended Reading: *The Long Awaited Meal* by Sue Nora Later.

Knock, knock!
Who's there?
Candy.
Candy who?
Candy waiter please bring me my order?

BILLY: Why are you holding that slice of bread?
WILLY: *Because I'd like to propose a toast.*

Recommended Reading: *I Like Garlic* by
I. Malone.

'Waiter, waiter, this coffee tastes like mud.'
'That's because it was only ground this morning.'

Recommended Reading: *The Restaurant Guide*
by Knife and Fork.

Where can you see a man-eating fish?
At a sea-food restaurant.

'Waiter, waiter, this soup tastes like dishwater.'
'How would you know, sir?'

Knock, knock!
Who's there?
Dismay.
Dismay who?
Dismay be a posh restaurant, but the food tastes awful.

What did the duck say to the waiter?
'Would you mind putting this meal on my bill?'

Recommended Reading: *The Underpaid Waiters* by General Strike.

What is a flying saucer?
A dish that's out of this world.

'Waiter, waiter, there's a bird in my soup.'
'Well, you did ask for bird's nest soup.'

Recommended Reading: *The Hungry Man* by I. C. Food.

What type of plate do skeletons eat off?
Bone china.

Knock, knock!
Who's there?
Bean.
Bean who?
Bean looking forward to eating at this restaurant
for ages.

Did you hear about the waiter who fell into a
barrel of beer?
He came to a bitter end.

Why don't violinists eat at restaurants?
Because they fiddle with their food.

Knock, knock!
Who's there?
Noah.
Noah who?
Noah any good restaurants?

CUSTOMER: Will you join me in a glass of lager?
BARMAN: *No thank you — I don't think we'll both fit in.*

How do you recognise a vampire at a restaurant?
He's the one with the cape on.

What did the boy maggot say to the girl maggot?
'What's a nice girl like you doing in a joint like this?'

MR SNOOTY: I expect it's quite difficult to eat your soup with that moustache.
MR TOOTY: *Yes — it's quite a strain.*

'Waiter, waiter, do you serve crabs?'
'Sit down, we serve anybody.'

Knock, knock!
Who's there?
Gorilla.
Gorilla who?
Gorilla me a piece of toast, I'm starving.

Can waiters jump higher than restaurants?
Yes — restaurants can't jump.

Knock, knock!
Who's there?
Egbert.
Egbert who?
Egbert no bacon, please.

BEN: I had roast boar here last night.
LEN: *Was it wild?*
BEN: Well, it wasn't very pleased.

Recommended Reading: *Indigestion* by Tommy Ache.

'Waiter, waiter, there's a fly in my soup.'
'That's not a fly, it's the last customer — the chef used to be a witch doctor.'

Knock, knock!
Who's there?
Dishes.
Dishes who?
Dishes terrible food.

Recommended Reading: *The Cracked Glass* by Ivor Wetfoot.

Why don't Chinamen eat soup?
Because they can't get enough on their chopsticks.

'Waiter, waiter, what's in the gold soup?'
'Carrots, sir.'

'Waiter , waiter, there's a fly in my soup!'
'That's because the chef used to be a tailor.'

'Waiter, waiter, this food is terrible — call the manager.'
'He won't eat it either, sir.'

What did the little pig say when the chef cut off his tail?
'This is the end of me!'

Recommended Reading: *A Table For Ten* by Major Booking.

Knock, knock!
Who's there?
Bison.
Bison who?
Pudding bison.

What type of monkeys make the best wine?
Grey apes.

'Waiter, waiter, there's a twig in my soup.'
'Just a moment, sir, I'll call the branch manager.'

A Whole Bag of Scraps

What room has no walls, no windows and no doors?
A mushroom.

What do you get if you cross a cow with a camel?
Lumpy milkshakes.

What type of motorbike should you use to cook an egg?
A scrambler.

How did the cannibal know the missionary had been eaten?
He had inside information.

What kind of biscuit can fly?
A plane one.

What do you call someone who steals pigs?
A hamburglar.

1ST CANNIBAL: Am I late for dinner?
2ND CANNIBAL: *Yes, everyone's eaten.*

Why wouldn't the orange go?
Because it ran out of juice.

What do you get if you cross a duck with a cow?
A milk float.

JERRY: I'd like some raw meat, lumpy potatoes
   and burnt gravy, please.
DINNER LADY: *I couldn't possibly give you that.*
JERRY: Why not? That's what you gave me
   yesterday.

Knock, knock!
Who's there?
Carmen.
Carmen who?
Carmen get it!

Why can't idiots raise chickens?
Because they plant the eggs too deep.

Recommended Reading: *School Dinners* by General Illness.

'Why do you want to be a baker?'
'So I can loaf around.'

What games do cannibals like to play?
Swallow the leader.

Why do idiots eat biscuits?
Because they're crackers.

Knock, knock!
Who's there?
Cows.
Cows who?
Cows go moo, not who.

How can you tell if an elephant has been in your fridge?
From the footprints in the butter.

Why is a banana like a jumper?
Because they're both easy to slip on.

Where do you go to learn how to make ice-cream?
To a sundae school.

What do you call a dinner lady with two bananas in her ears?
Anything you like because she can't hear you.

Recommended Reading: *School Rock Cakes* by Buster Tooth.

Where do tough chickens come from?
Hard-boiled eggs.

Knock, knock!
Who's there?
Lionel.
Lionel who?
Lionel roar if you don't feed him.

What do cannibals like for breakfast?
Buttered host.

What do French children say when they've eaten just their school dinner?
Mercy!'

Knock, knock!'
Who's there?
Ketchup.
Ketchup who?
Ketchup with me and I'll tell you.

Knock, knock!
Who's there?
Soup.
Soup who?
Soup-erman.

What do you call a monkey with a sweet tooth?
A meringue-outang.

Recommended Reading: *I Hate Margarine* by Roland Butter.

If there are two tomatoes on your plate, which one is the cowboy?
Neither — they're both redskins.

What can't you do if you put a five-tonne jelly in the fridge?
Close the door.

Recommended Reading: *How To Make Rock Cakes* by C. Ment.

What should you do for a starving cannibal?
Give him a hand.

What exam do horses take?
Hay levels.

What kind of biscuit lives at the South Pole?
A Penguin.

TEACHER: Eat all your greens — they're good for your complexion.
SALLY: *But I don't want a green complexion.*

What do you get if you cross a cake with a tin of baked beans?
A birthday cake that blows its own candles out.

KELLY: Once a week I like to bath in milk.
NELLY: *Pasteurized?*
KELLY: No, just up to my waist.

Recommended Reading: *Grow Your Own Rice* by Paddy Fields.

What do vegetarian cannibals eat?
Swedes.

Knock, knock!
Who's there?
Goose.
Goose who?
Goose who's come for dinner.

Recommended Reading: *Awful Food* by Willie Eatit.

'Doctor, doctor, I feel like an electric eel.'
'That's shocking.'

SALLY: Why do you keep a slice of bread in the middle of your joke book?
BILLY: *Because I like crumby jokes.*

Our school dinners are so bad even the dustbins have uclers.

Where do motorists stop to drink?
At a T-junction.

CANNIBAL BOY: Should you eat chicken legs with your fingers?
CANNIBAL TEACHER: *No — fingers should be eaten separately.*

Recommended Reading: *Seasickness* by Eva Lott.

LARRY: We're having my gran for Christmas dinner this year.
BARRY: *Really? We usually have turkey.*

What do you get if you cross a chicken with a cement mixer?
A brick-layer.

What do you get if you cross a witch with an ice-cube?
A cold spell.

What happened when the boy vampire met the girl vampire?
It was love at first bite.

Why don't people like Dracula?
Because he's a pain in the neck.

Knock, knock!
Who's there?
Dawn.
Dawn who?
Dawn forget you dinner money.

Recommended Reading: *Never Make A Dinner Lady Angry* by Sheila Tack.

Why did Mr and Mrs Mopp call their daughter Margarine?
Because they didn't have any but her.

Why couldn't the idiot make ice-cubes?
Because he lost the recipe.

How do you make an elephant stew?
Keep him waiting for hours.

What food turns without moving?
Milk — when it turns sour.

What should you give a sick elephant?
Plenty of room!

What do you get if you cross a cockerel with a poodle?
A cockerpoodledoo.

How do you recognize a miser's house?
It's the one with the teabags hanging on the line.

What do you get if you cross a dinner lady's brain with a piece of elastic?
A stretch of the imagination.

Business was so quiet at the sweet factory you could hear a cough drop.

Knock, knock!
Who's there?
Tina.
Tina who?
Tina tomatoes.

Why are dentists artistic?
Because they're good at drawing teeth.

When should you feed leaopard's milk to a baby?
When it's a baby leopard.

What do you get if you cross a dinner lady with a lion?
Very nervous children.

Why did Frankenstein's monster get indigestion?
Because he bolted his food down.

What do ghosts like to chew?
Booble gum.

What's stupid and yellow?
Thick custard.

How do you stop a fish smelling?
Put a peg on its nose.

What do you call an evil woman who lives by the sea?
A sand-witch.

What kind of birds lay electric eggs.
Battery hens.

What did the drunken chicken lay?
Scotch eggs.

Why did the milkmaid sit down?
Because she couldn't stand milking.

What do cannibals like for dinner?
Human beans and boiled legs followed by eyes cream.

Why did the baby biscuit cry?
Because his mother was a wafer so long.

What do you call an overweight pumpkin?
A plumpkin.

What did the lamb chop say to the maggot?
'You bore me.'

POSH BOY POTATO: I want to be just like Dickie Davis when I grow up.
POSH FATHER POTATO: *Don't be silly — he's just a common tater.*

How can you tell if there's an elephant hiding in
the school custard?
It's a little lumpier than usual.

What do you call a cow that gives no milk?
A udder failure.

What did the grape say when the elephant stood
on him?
Nothing — he just gave a little wine.

PATIENT: Doctor, doctor, I keep thinking I'm a
joint of ham.
DOCTOR: *Don't worry — I'll soon cure you.*

Knock, knock!
Who's there?
Juicy.
Juicy who?
Juicy what I saw?

What is white on the outside, grey on the inside and moves across the table very slowly?
A slug sandwich.

Knock, knock!
Who's there?
Duane.
Duane who?
Duane your basin and you can have some more soup.

Why did the cook smack the sausage?
Because it spat in the pan.

Why do dogs eat raw meat?
Because they don't know how to cook.

Knock, knock!
Who's there?
Waiter.
Waiter who?
Waiter 'till you try my pudding.

Did you hear about the stupid woodworm?
He was found in a brick.

Recommended Reading: *Salmonella* by Mike Robe.

What happened to the man who put his false teeth
in backwards?
He ate himself.

Why did the baker ask for a pay rise?
Because he needed more dough.

What is a ghost's favourite soup?
Scream of tomato.

What does a polite vampire say?
'Fang you very much.'

Did you hear about the idiot who ate a sofa and
three chairs?
He had a suite tooth.

Why did the cow jump over the moon?
Because the farmer had such cold hands.

Why did the idiot eat candles?
For a little light refreshment.

Knock, knock!
Who's there?
Kipper.
Kipper who?
Kipper your hands to yourself!

What do you feed parrots with?
Polyfilla.

Which creatures didn't go into the Ark in pairs?
The maggots — they went in apples.

Knock, knock!
Who's there?
Cook.
Cook who?
That's the first one I've heard this year.

Recommended Reading: *School Dinners Make Me Sick* by Eileen Dover.

PATIENT: Doctor, doctor, I keep thinking I'm a chicken.
DOCTOR: *Gracious me, how long has this been going on?*
PATIENT: Seven years.
DOCTOR: *Seven years? Why didn't you come sooner?*
PATIENT: My wife couldn't do without the eggs.

What is 300 metres high and wobbles?
The Trifle Tower.

What do you call a drunken ghost?
A methylated spirit.

BILLY: That new boy in our class does bird impressions.

WILLY: *So what? I know lots of people who do bird impressions.*

BILLY: Not like him – he eats worms.

How do you make a Swiss roll?
Push him off an alp.

Knock, knock!
Who's there?
Turnip.
Turnip who?
Turnip the heat – it is freezing in here.

What happened to the scientist who swallowed a piece of uranium?
He got atomic ache.

Why are 4840 square yards like a bad tooth?
Because they're an acre.

What do you get if you cross an egg with a barrel of gunpowder?
A boom-meringue.

'Doctor, doctor, I feel like a spoon.'
'Just sit down and don't stir.'

Why couldn't Batman go fishing?
Because Robin ate all the worms.

What goes, 'A B C D E F G H I J K L M N O P Q R S T U V W X Y Z, slurp!'?
A greedy boy eating alphabet soup.

How do you start a pudding race?
Sago.

How do witches like their eggs?
Terror-fried.

Did you hear about the boy who drank eight bottles of lemonade?
He burped 7-Up.

What do you get if you cross Dracula with a hot dog?
A fangfurter.

LENNY: Should I use my left hand to stir my drink or should I use my right hand?
TEACHER: *Neither — you should use a spoon.*

Who is the thirstiest person in the world?
The one who drinks Canada Dry.

What's the Queen's favourite drink?
Royal tea.

What kind of biscuit robs banks?
A safe-cracker.

When is a door nice to eat?
When it's jammed.

Knock, knock!
Who's there?
Cod.
Cod who?
Cod-bye, so-long, because that's the end of the book!

Other great reads **from Red Fox**

Further Red Fox titles that you might enjoy reading are listed on the following pages. They are available in bookshops or they can be ordered directly from us.

If you would like to order books, please send this form and the money due to:

ARROW BOOKS, BOOKSERVICE BY POST, PO BOX 29, DOUGLAS, ISLE OF MAN, BRITISH ISLES. Please enclose a cheque or postal order made out to Arrow Books Ltd for the amount due, plus 30p per book for postage and packing to a maximum of £3.00, both for orders within the UK. For customers outside the UK, please allow 35p per book.

NAME _____

ADDRESS _____

_____

Please print clearly.

Whilst every effort is made to keep prices low, it is sometimes necessary to increase cover prices at short notice. If you are ordering books by post, to save delay it is advisable to phone to confirm the correct price. The number to ring is THE SALES DEPARTMENT 071 (if outside London) 973 9700.

Other great reads ✐ *from* **Red Fox**

THE SNIFF STORIES Ian Whybrow

Things just keep happening to Ben Moore. It's dead hard avoiding disaster when you've got to keep your street cred with your mates *and* cope with a family of oddballs at the same time. There's his appalling 2½ year old sister, his scatty parents who are into healthy eating and animal rights and, worse than all of these, there's Sniff! If only Ben could just get on with his scientific experiments and his attempt at a world beating *Swampbeast* score . . . but there's no chance of that while chaos is just around the corner.

ISBN 0 09 975040 6   £2.99

J.B. SUPERSLEUTH Joan Davenport

James Bond is a small thirteen-year-old with spots and spectacles. But with a name like that, how can he help being a supersleuth?

It all started when James and 'Polly' (Paul) Perkins spotted a teacher's stolen car. After that, more and more mysteries needed solving. With the case of the Arabian prince, the Murdered Model, the Bonfire Night Murder and the Lost Umbrella, JB's reputation at Moorside Comprehensive soars.

But some of the cases aren't quite what they seem . . .

ISBN 0 09 971780 8   £2.99

Other great reads from **Red Fox**

The latest and funniest joke books are from Red Fox!

THE OZONE FRIENDLY JOKE BOOK
Kim Harris, Chris Langham, Robert Lee,
Richard Turner

What's green and highly dangerous?
How do you start a row between conservationists?
What's green and can't be rubbed out?

Green jokes for green people (non-greens will be pea-green when they see how hard you're laughing), bags and bags of them (biodegradable of course).

All the jokes in this book are printed on environmentally friendly paper and every copy you buy will help GREENPEACE save our planet.

* David Bellamy with a machine gun.
* Pour oil on troubled waters.
* The Indelible hulk.

ISBN 0 09 973190 8   £1.99

THE HAUNTED HOUSE JOKE BOOK
John Hegarty

There are skeletons in the scullery . . .
Beasties in the bath . . .
There are spooks in the sitting room
And jokes to make you laugh . . .

Search your home and see if we are right. Then come back, sit down and shudder to the hauntingly funny and eerily rib-rattling jokes in this book.

ISBN 0 09 9621509   £1.99

Other great reads from Red Fox

AMAZING ORIGAMI FOR CHILDREN
Steve and Megumi Biddle

Origami is an exciting and easy way to make toys, decorations and all kinds of useful things from folded paper.

Use leftover gift paper to make a party hat and a fancy box. Or create a colourful lorry, a pretty rose and a zoo full of origami animals. There are over 50 fun projects in Amazing Origami.

Following Steve and Megumi's step-by-step instructions and clear drawings, you'll amaze your friends and family with your magical paper creations.

ISBN 0 09 966180 2   £5.99

MAGICAL STRING   Steve and Megumi Biddle

With only a loop of string you can make all kinds of shapes, puzzles and games. Steve and Megumi Biddle provide all the instructions and diagrams that are needed to create their amazing string magic in another of their inventive and absorbing books.

ISBN 0 09 964470 3   £2.50